Little Lion Goes For Gold

Eight little boys knelt in a row
Waiting for the whistle's blow
Coach Clafbert Clump paced to and fro
"On your mark! Get set! Go!"

The boys sped off
The race was on
One little boy just would not run
Seven ran with all their might
Little Lion stood stiff with fright

"Run, Little Lion!"
Cried Coach Claffie
Little Lion's legs felt like jelly
"Come on, Little Lion
Go! Go! Go!"
Little Lion's legs said
"No! No! No!"

HM

All the boys sped down the track
Little Lion was way at the back
Legs were pounding
Arms were pumping
Little Lion was huffing and puffing

Seven boys finished fast
Little Lion came in last
He crawled home and said
"I'm done"
"I'm sorry, Papa.
I just can't run"

Papa said
"Don't give up so fast
Quitting is worse than coming last
If at first you don't win, then
You have to try and try again"

"Every race is a new test
Always try your very best
Just keep going
Never stop
Soon you'll make it to the top"

HM

Little Lion went back to school
Thinking about Papa's rule
He tried his hardest in the race
And this time he took fourth place!

Little Lion ran race after race
A smile lit up Coach Claffie's face
"Little Lion, you're gaining steam
I'm putting you on the track team"

Little Lion went to bed
Track stars running 'round his head
"I may be the smallest guy
But I'm going to try, try, try"

He sprinted off to school each day
He ran home the longest way
He ran to and from the store
He ran and ran and ran some more

Saturday he went to the track
He started off with jumping jacks
Push ups, pull ups
Chin ups, squats
He skipped
He stretched
He jumped
He hopped
His little legs were growing faster
His little body growing stronger
Papa said "That's it, Little Lion
You're training like a champion!"

Left, right, left, right
He ran all day
He ran all night
With every step, he sang along
Making up a brand new song

"I'm getting ready for my race
I'm making sure I win first place
I'm going to the Stadium
I'm going to run, run, run"

Everybody on his lane
Came to watch Little Lion train
They sang along to the beat
Tapped out by his flying feet

"Run, run, run, run, run
Watch Little Lion run
He runs with his heart and soul
We know he'll bring home gold
He's quick like Quarrie
Bad like Bolt
He's magic like Merlene
Strong as Asafa
Fast as Veronica
The best we've ever seen"

S.L.I.M

HM
HOLY
MOTHER
TRACK

Before long, the big day had come
There it was – the Stadium
Friends, fans, parents, teachers
Filled the Grand Stand
And the bleachers

Every school had sent its team
All of them with just one dream
To be the best school in the land
To reign atop the medal stand

Little Lion took his place
In the 50 metre race
A tingly thrill tickled his spine
As he stepped on the starting line
He felt the magic and the power
Of all the greats who'd run before
His little legs felt strong and steady
He sighed
And smiled
And said
"I'm ready"

RUN!
HOLY MOTHER
HM

Eight little boys knelt in a row
Waiting for the whistle's blow
They called their names
One by one
"Lane four: Nick Nylon
Lane five: Zachariah Zion
Also known as Little Lion"

"On your mark! Get set! Go!"
Little Lion flew
Like an arrow from a bow
Nick Nylon sprinted by his side
Little Lion matched him
Stride for stride

The sky was blue
The sun was bright
Little Lion ran with all his might
He sped ahead with one last burst
And crossed the finish line in first!

Myah Moore and Kayla King
Led the happy fans in cheering
The whole stadium sang along
To Little Lion's running song

"I worked so hard to win my race
I'm so glad I won first place!
I'm here in the Stadium
I'm having fun, fun, fun"

HM
HM

"Run, run, run, run, run
Watch Little Lion run
He ran with his heart and soul
Little Lion won the gold!"

THE END